Xtraordinary People

Written by Kate Griggs
Illustrated by Steven Woods

Foreword

Question: What do Whoopi Goldberg, Richard Branson, and Roald Dahl have in common?

Answer: They're all famous people with dyslexia.

When we're dyslexic, we think slightly differently than those who are not dyslexic, and that can be a really good thing. While everyone is naturally good at some things, we might find a lot of things we're better at than our friends who are not dyslexic. But we might also find certain things tricky at school (more so than our friends). That's because school tests and exams typically measure the very things we find challenging, and this can make us (and others) mistakenly believe we're not as smart as our peers, when we absolutely are.

"Dyslexia is a great part of how your brain works and everybody's brain works differently. There is nothing wrong…there is just everything that is so right."
– HRH Princess Beatrice of York
STORYTELLER. "PEOPLE" PERSON.

As many as 1 in 5 people are dyslexic, and while we may struggle with spelling, reading, or memorizing facts, we often perform above average on Dyslexic Thinking skills like communicating, reasoning, visualizing, and creative problem solving. These skills aren't ones we're normally tested on in school, but they are some of the most valuable and sought after skills worldwide.

So the most important thing we can all do for every dyslexic child is to find out what they are passionate about (and maybe already Xtraordinarily good at) and help them to do lots of it, because there lies the formula for unleashing their unique Dyslexic Thinking abilities.

Happy reading!

Kate x

What makes us Xtraordinary?

People **made by dyslexia** can be very good at certain things. We say it's what makes us **Xtraordinary**.

With this Xtraordinary way of thinking, it's very important to remember what we're Xtraordinarily good at, and not worry too much about our challenges. With some extra help and lots of practice, we can learn to do these challenging things as well as, and sometimes even better than, anyone else.

Once we're good at something, we usually enjoy doing it so much that we keep practicing and practicing, until eventually we become Xtraordinarily good at it!

Dyslexic Challenges

People **made by dyslexia** find some things difficult. Some people call them our **dyslexic challenges**. We think a little differently from people who are not dyslexic. This Xtraordinary way of thinking means that some things are much harder for us than for people without dyslexia, especially school work!

Things like learning to read, write, and spell...

or remembering lots of facts and figures...

or concentrating and following instructions.

Tests are particularly tricky for us, as they are often a combination of all of these things! When we find things difficult it can make us feel embarrassed, or even stupid... and we are absolutely **not** stupid!

Xtraordinary Jobs

When dyslexic people grow up, we can use our Xtraordinary way of thinking to help us become Xtraordinarily good at our jobs... usually jobs we love.

There are dyslexic people doing all sorts of Xtraordinary jobs, such as...

firefighters, doctors, and nurses...

entrepreneurs, musicians, and actors...

and even rocket scientists and investigators!

Being made by dyslexia can make us into Xtraordinary people!

There are seven types of Xtraordinary people...

Storytellers

Makers

Entertainers

Movers

Imaginers

Questioners

"People" People

Which type of Xtraordinary person are you? Or are you a mixture?

Storytellers

Storytellers just love stories! Many enjoy creating their own stories, and some can be very persuasive. Some **Storytellers** like finding out all about the world around them and sharing what they have learned with others. **Storytellers** love to listen to stories and watch them on TV.

When they grow up, Storytellers often become...

journalists, teachers...

writers, filmmakers...

politicians, or campaigners.

Makers

Makers really love to make things! They enjoy building with bricks and putting together jigsaw puzzles. Some **Makers** like to cook, craft, or make models. Some **Makers** create fantastic art and paintings, while others prefer using technology and gadgets.

When they grow up, Makers often become...

architects, craftspeople...

chefs, designers...

gardeners, artists, or programmers.

Entertainers

Entertainers love to entertain! Some learn to play musical instruments, and others love to sing or dance. Some **Entertainers** love to act and enjoy performing and putting on shows. Other **Entertainers** are jokers and love making people laugh. Some **Entertainers** are excited when they hear new music and want other people to hear it too.

When they grow up, Entertainers often become...

actors, musicians...

comedians, salespeople...

PR people, or presenters.

Movers

Movers love to move! They are often fidgety and are always on the go. Some **Movers** love to do daring things like skateboarding, climbing, or extreme sports. Some **Movers** keep active by playing team sports or exercising regularly. Others like to do gymnastics, move their bodies to music, or dance.

When they grow up, Movers often become...

 sports coaches, athletes...

dancers, musicians...

 choreographers, or firefighters.

Imaginers

Imaginers love to imagine! They enjoy daydreaming and playing at make-believe. Some like creating imaginary worlds and making up games, pretending to be superheroes, or having magical powers. **Imaginers** love to fantasize and invent amazing things that don't even exist yet!

When they grow up, Imaginers often become...

Questioners

Questioners love questions! They constantly ask **Why?** or **Why not? Questioners** are naturally curious and inquisitive. Some love to challenge the rules. Others have an answer for everything and love explaining things. **Questioners** also like to solve problems that others can't.

When they grow up, Questioners often become...

detectives, investigators...

entrepreneurs, journalists...

writers, or changemakers.

"People" People

"People" People love people! They love helping and taking care of their friends. Some are very interested in others and some enjoy organizing everyone. Some **"People" People** are peacemakers, and others are leaders. **"People" People** often understand how others are feeling. Many **"People" People** are quite shy, but some are not shy at all.

When they grow up, "People" People often become...

nurses, doctors...

managers, TV hosts...

teachers, or healthcare workers.

That's why...

People **made by dyslexia** should remember what we are good at and not spend too long worrying about those things we find challenging. With help and practice we can learn to do challenging things well enough and do things we are good at extremely well!

When dyslexic people grow up, we can use our Xtraordinary way of thinking to do Xtraordinary things. In fact, people **made by dyslexia** have made some of the greatest inventions of all time, such as the airplane, the lightbulb, and the telephone!

You see, being "made by dyslexia" really does make YOU an Xtraordinary person!

The Xtraordinary People Quiz

What type of Xtraordinary person do you think you are?
What do you love to do? What are you naturally good at?

Storytellers

- You love to invent stories and characters or listen to stories.
- You're good at persuading people to do things.
- You're great at explaining things.

Makers

- You love building all sorts of amazing creations, or doing jigsaw puzzles.
- You enjoy drawing, painting, and making things.
- You're great at building worlds online.

Entertainer

- You love to sing or play a musical instrument.
- You really feel alive when you dance or put on a show.
- You can be funny and make people laugh.

Movers
- You're always on the move, and you think best when moving.
- You're happiest doing sports or exercise.
- You spend lots of time practicing sports.

Imaginers
- You're a fantastic daydreamer.
- You love making up games, or can spend hours playing roles and let's pretend.
- You love thinking up and inventing new things.

Questioners
- You ask questions like **What if?** and **Why not?**
- You often challenge the way things are done.
- You love to solve problems, explain things, or find out how things work.

"People" people
- You're good at understanding how others feel.
- You know how and when to cheer up your friends, and helping people makes you feel happy.
- You're good at organizing things.

The important thing is discovering what makes you Xtraordinary and then doing lots of it. Make the most of your Xtraordinary skills!

Famous people "made by dyslexia"

Space scientists
"Kids should have a dream and aim as high as they can imagine. I dreamed of reaching the stars, and by having that dream I've done so much more than I would have ever thought possible."
Dr. Maggie Aderin-Pocock MBE—Scientist and educator
IMAGINER. STORYTELLER. QUESTIONER.

Spies
"Across all our missions, we have dyslexic people. From the best mathematicians to our most talented engineers and analysts, I see dyslexics among every one of those."
Jeremy Fleming—"Spy Boss"
(Director of GCHQ, UK intelligence service)
QUESTIONER.

Actors
"You may not be a brilliant speller, or a fast reader, but you will learn how to read, and you will learn as much spelling as you need to know, and you will be brilliant at different things."
Keira Knightley—Film actor
IMAGINER. ENTERTAINER.

Dancers
"My mother sent me to dance class when I was five. It took me a while to fall in love with it, but as soon as I realized I had a strength, that changed my whole attitude to everything else I approached."
Darcey Bussell—Ballerina
MOVER. ENTERTAINER.

Athletes

"Dyslexia has given me the work ethic to stick with things even if things aren't going well. I always wanted to be a rugby player and I'm extremely lucky I got to that position."

Chris Robshaw—Captain of the England Rugby team
MOVER.

Dinosaur hunters

"Since I was ten, I wanted to study dinosaurs. I wasn't sure how I was going to do it because I had bad grades, but I never doubted it could be done."

Jack Horner—Paleontologist/adviser for Jurassic Park
IMAGINER. QUESTIONER.

Chefs

"There are different types of intelligence and everyone has the ability to be brilliant…kids need to find their inner genius and confidence. I think my strength is a complete obsession to empower and teach people to cook."

Jamie Oliver—Chef/TV presenter
MAKER. STORYTELLER. IMAGINER.

Entrepreneurs

"I simply wouldn't be where I am today if I wasn't dyslexic. In the real world, dyslexia can be a huge advantage…Many of the world's great entrepreneurs and inventors are dyslexic. Thomas Edison illuminated our lives, Henry Ford made cars accessible to all, and Steve Jobs gave us pocket computers."

Richard Branson—Co-founder of Virgin
IMAGINER. QUESTIONER. "PEOPLE" PERSON.

Author Kate Griggs
Illustrator Steven Woods

Editors Becca Arlington, Penny Morris
Designers Eleanor Bates, Helen Chapman
US Editor Kris Hirschmann
Sensitivity Reader Lisa Davis
Managing Art Editor Anna Hall
Jacket Coordinator Elin Woosnam
Production Editor Gillian Reid
Production Controller Jack Matts
Publisher Francesca Young

First American Edition, 2025
Published in the United States by DK Publishing,
a division of Penguin Random House LLC
1745 Broadway, 20th Floor, New York, NY 10019

Kate Griggs has asserted her right to be
identified as the author of this work
Text and Illustrations copyright © Kate Griggs 2025
Copyright in the layouts and design
of the Work will vest in the Publisher
25 26 27 28 29 10 9 8 7 6 5 4 3 2 1
001–343975–Apr/2025

All rights reserved.
Without limiting the rights under the copyright reserved above, no part of this publication may be reproduced, stored in or introduced into a retrieval system, or transmitted, in any form, or by any means (electronic, mechanical, photocopying, recording, or otherwise), without the prior written permission of the copyright owner.
Published in Great Britain by Dorling Kindersley Limited

A catalog record for this book
is available from the Library of Congress.
ISBN 978-0-5939-5929-9

DK books are available at special discounts when purchased in bulk for sales promotions, premiums, fund-raising, or educational use.
For details, contact: DK Publishing Special Markets,
1745 Broadway, 20th Floor, New York, NY 10019
SpecialSales@dk.com

Printed and bound in China

www.dk.com

This book was made with Forest Stewardship Council™ certified paper—one small step in DK's commitment to a sustainable future. Learn more at www.dk.com/uk/information/sustainability

Watch these Xtraordinary people and many others tell their stories on our website, and find lots of helpful information to inform and inspire you too.

ABOUT THE AUTHOR

Kate Griggs is the founder of **Made By Dyslexia**, a charity that works to help everyone understand the Xtraordinary strengths dyslexia gives us. She, and everyone in her family, is dyslexic (except her dog, Griff). She is a **Questioner** and a **Storyteller**. Find out about her wonderful work at
www.madebydyslexia.org